Grassroots:101

The Fundamentals of political success

The Advanced Guide to Grassroots Politics

Grassroots 101 Training Series

Level 3: Advanced

DrewMcKissick.com
Campaigns, Opinions & Activism

Welcome to the Grassroots101 Training Series

This book is the third volume in a three part series that seeks to demystify the political system and give a basic understanding of some of the more fundamental techniques that can help you achieve political success.

The purpose of this edition is to provide a "how to" for the more advanced levels of political involvement relating to:

1) *Advanced lobbying*
2) *Campaigns and elections*
3) *Communications*
4) *Parliamentary procedure*
5) *Volunteer management*

Hopefully you and others you know will find it useful and will then part from your hard earned money for Levels One and Two! (All part of my evil plan)

Level One provides basic "how to" guidance for the beginner's level of political activity relating to:

1) *Grassroots Opportunities*
2) *Church Organization*
3) *Precinct Organization*
4) *Online Organization*
5) *Being an Effective Volunteer*

Level Two covers the more intermediate levels of political activity relating to:

1) *Political Parties*
2) *The Legislative Process*
3) *Basic Lobbying*
4) *Effective Confrontation*
5) *Election Voter Guides*
6) *Newsletters*
7) *Dealing with the Media*

You can always find links to these and other helpful political resources at DrewMcKissick.com. You can also connect with me on Twitter at: @DrewMcKissick. Rather stay in touch via email? Then click here and subscribe via Feedburner.

TABLE OF CONTENTS

INTRODUCTION

"In a democracy, he who does not take an active interest and participate in public affairs is worthless". – Pericles

Are you "worthless"? How important are you to the success of the things that you believe?

Today our society needs conservatives to be willing to get involved and play an active role in our democracy like never before. To matter to the things that they believe. The good news is that you don't have to be a politician in order to make a difference. You just have to be willing to participate and then let your voice be heard.

Conservative grassroots activism can change policy and influence decisions from the local school boards all the way to Washington, DC – but it depends on how diligent you are. If we are going to be successful, we have to commit to doing what Ronald Reagan called "the hard work of freedom". And that work includes community, social and political action. *And effective activism begins with knowledge*.

The purpose of the Grassroots Training Series is not to be exhaustive, (that's another book!), but rather to cover the highlights and break down the complexities of the political system and help the novice activist understand how to become more effective. To better equip you to make a difference at all levels of government.

The two things that truly determine how effective individuals can be are their knowledge of the system and their willingness to participate. This series addresses the first one. The second is up to you.

_____

SECTION 1: ADVANCED LOBBYING

"Ten people who speak make more noise than ten thousand who are silent." - Napoleon

Our government revolves around lobbying. Not just in the sense of paid lobbyists in expensive suits, but rather that our form of government makes every citizen a potential lobbyist. People in other countries don't enjoy the same opportunities that we do to have a direct impact on government. For all of its flaws, American democracy is superior because it allows for the full participation of all of its citizens. And that includes lobbying.

This section is designed to build on the lessons taught in the Basic Lobbying section of Level 2 of the Grassroots Training Series. If you have not reviewed that material, or have little experience with lobbying, you may want to obtain a copy of that manual, as it provides the proper groundwork for the more advanced methods outlined in this section.

Picking a fight

...is this really necessary?

Is the battle worth fighting? That's the question you need to ask before you get started on any lobbying plan. In other words, choose your fights carefully. Some have larger consequences than others, and some may cost more in terms of resources. You will never have the manpower or the financial resources to fight every battle, so choose carefully.

> ## Consider the following:
>
> - *Is this fight consistent with the overall mission of your group?*
> - *What resources will be used on this effort?*
> - *Will a victory in this fight advance the conservative cause?*
> - *Can you win?*
> - *Will a loss lay groundwork for future success?*

Research

...do your homework!

Good research is the foundation of good lobbying. But good research can require a lot of work. Elected officials don't have the time to follow the nuances of every piece of legislation, yet they are required to put their name, reputation, and possibly their career on the line by casting a vote. As a result, good information is invaluable. <u>The rule is: do the work for them.</u> A legislator can't expect to know everything and doesn't have the time to learn. They are forced to be generalists. So part of the job of lobbying is be an expert on the issues you advocate.

> ## Information All Public Official Need:
> - *The details of a proposal*
> - *How it changes current law or the status quo*
> - *How those changes will impact their constituents*

Without this knowledge, they can only hope and pray that they don't accidentally stumble into a politically explosive situation. Where do government officials find the types of information they need to make decisions? A good bit of it comes from educated constituents who have done their homework. <u>The more you understand the details of a legislative proposal, (how it will change the status quo and what impact it will have on your community), the more valuable you are to your elected officials.</u> They are moving quickly and handling dozens of issues at a time, and they are always searching for people who can help them understand how the proposals before them will impact their constituents.

The point is that you should use this reality to your advantage. <u>Aim to become a valuable informational resource for the officials you need to influence.</u> So how do you do that? Begin by contacting those already actively working on the issue. Many of the questions you will have as you begin can be answered by someone who already has some background knowledge. If these sources don't provide the details you need, remember that most public offices, whether local, state or federal, are required by law to open their records to citizens under the Freedom of Information Act. While this is usually done without any resistance, keep in mind that your attitude in dealing with the public officials who hold these records can affect how cooperative they may be. Bureaucrats aren't always the most helpful people in the world.

Becoming an Issue Expert:

- *Call those who are already active on the issue at hand and pick their brains*

- *Compile a list of those supporting and opposing the issue*

- *Research the basics of the issue (online, at the library or govt. office)*

- *Start a news clipping file on the issue, (online services like Google and Google News Alerts make it easy)*

- *Keep track of positions taken by elected officials on the issue*

- *Build coalitions of like-minded people to work on the issue*

Remember that information is power. Most legislation is passed by legislators holding only scant knowledge of what it contains. They will usually be grateful if you provide them with details of what a proposal will do.

Coalition Building

...a little help from my friends

Most national level lobbying is done through coalitions. Lobbyists figured out long ago that they could be much more productive if they distributed the work load and shared intelligence. Likewise, your lobbying efforts will be more effective if you can convince others to join you in a team effort. Lobbying coalitions come in all shapes and sizes, but the primary types are as follows:

- *Informal Coalitions:* These are coalitions that are formed to share intelligence and "keep each other in the loop". Meeting with your natural allies on a regular basis will help to decrease back-biting and build trust. You could meet weekly or monthly, in person, or by conference call.

- *Natural Allies/Strange Bedfellows:* Work with your natural allies in coalitions (like-minded groups and elected officials), but also look for opportunities to work with those that you normally don't associate with, (i.e., "strange-bedfellows" coalitions). Sometimes these partners work on

4

different issues, and sometimes they work on opposite sides of the fence. Such groups are hard to form. Our natural inclination is to work with our friends, not those we don't know, and certainly not our enemies. However, try to overcome these feelings when you find an issue that you can unite on because these groups can be *very powerful!* They offer you credibility by appealing across ideological lines, as well as providing access to additional sets of legislative contacts.

- ***Inside/Outside Coalition:*** The best coalitions combine grassroots groups on the outside with legislative leaders on the inside. Legislators are privy to inside information you might not know unless you work with them, and they have a better grasp of the ins and outs of the legislative process. So the first step is to recruit a legislator that can help you from the inside.

> ## What to Look for in a Legislative Ally:
>
> - ***Belief:*** *Does the legislator really believe in your issue?*
>
> - ***Energy:*** *Will that person work hard?*
>
> - ***Power:*** *Is the legislator on the right committee? Does he have seniority? Please note that belief and energy trump "power". It is better to have a lowly freshman who will devote a lot of time to the cause than a committee chairman who is merely sympathetic.*
>
> - ***You know them well:*** *Legislators don't often do favors for strangers. If the right person is not someone you know, get to know them.*
>
> - ***Reputation:*** *Does the legislator have the respect of colleagues, or do they view him or her as extremist or inflammatory?*

MISSION STATEMENT

It is very important to have a written mission statement for the group. It clearly sets out the purpose for everyone to see, agree to and abide by, and it also lets potential new recruits know what they are joining. Most important, it provides an anchor to refer to when making and evaluating plans. If something doesn't serve the mission, then you don't do it.

5

TASKS TO ACCOMPLISH

Coalitions are formed in order to take coordinated action. Some highly structured, formal coalitions even raise money and hire staff; but you don't need to be that large to be effective, just organized. <u>In the end, the important point is that all of the work gets done, not how.</u>

If the group is large enough, one option is to assign each task to a subcommittee. Each subcommittee chairman could then serve on a steering committee that sets the agenda and makes decisions for the whole group.

Fundamental Tasks of Lobbying Coalitions:

- *Lobbying*
- *Research*
- *Grassroots organization*
- *Communications (coordination)*
- *Recruiting (of other allies)*

LEADERSHIP

Someone has to be in charge. This means that selecting a chairman and establishing rules are important. You may want to pick a chairman who is strong and who can speak on behalf of the group without obtaining prior approval. Or you may want a chairman who merely convenes meetings and makes sure the discussion doesn't wander. Here are some thoughts to keep in mind:

Attributes of Successful Coalition Chairman:

- *Everyone trusts him or her*
- *Gets along with everyone*
- *Will not abuse power for personal benefit*
- *Knows how to run a structured meeting*

6

GROUND RULES

Be sure to establish a clear set of ground rules regarding how the group makes decisions on what actions to take. Without a good upfront understanding of how this happens, you run the risk of having the group splinter when a decision is made that others may disagree with.

Here are some examples of how the process can work:

- *No action without group consensus,* **(unanimity):** (*Advantage*: may be the only way to handle "hot potato" issues; Disadvantage: hard to move forward)

- *Majority vote or two-thirds vote:* (*Advantage:* defines what consensus means, other than unanimity; *Disadvantage:* for those groups outvoted, it can put their organization's goals at odds with the group's goals)

- *Opt out:* If there is a conflict of goals, all groups that can, should take coordinated action. Those groups that can't would disqualify themselves from that action item only. (*Advantage:* a way of solving the above problem; *Disadvantage:* the group does not act at full strength)

KEYS TO SUCCESS

- *Work with one another:* Many group dynamics are always in play, but remember, you are on the same side. Try and put egos and personality conflicts aside.

- *Give people ownership:* The earlier allies are recruited into the group, the better. They understand the context and feel that they are part of the decision making process. People who feel they had a part in "the plan" are more likely to help carry it out.

- *Make sure the meetings go well:* There is a natural enthusiasm when starting a new endeavor, whether it is starting a new lobbying coalition or a new grassroots organization. <u>Unless sustained action replaces the initial enthusiasm, the group will die off.</u> On the other hand, if an organization becomes the place where "things are really happening," people will want to join. While people are busy and don't want to waste their time with "another meeting," they will flock to be part of the action for something that's really working.

- *Develop a culture of activism:* Let everyone who wants to join the group know that they should not join unless they are prepared to volunteer for action items. <u>Every meeting should include action items</u> that the members can volunteer for, as well a review of action items from the previous

7

meeting to make sure they were done or get status updates. This brings a sense of accountability to the group.

TARGETING VOTES

Where will you spend your time? While all legislators should get a letter stating your position, some legislators definitely will be with you, and some definitely against. It's not worth spending a lot of your time lobbying either group. Your job is to focus on the votes in the middle – the "swing" votes. This requires research, organization, careful note taking, and close coordination with your allies. Use the following guidelines:

- *Develop a target list:* Find past votes on identical or similar issues that can help predict future behavior. Also, the general impressions from lobbyists as well as your leaders inside the legislature should be put into the mix. Lastly, depending on whether legislators are up for reelection, the narrowness of their former election victories may be a factor as well, (they all want to get re-elected!).

- *Organize the list:* Most lobbyists rate legislators on a 1 to 5 scale, (1 = absolutely with you, 2 = leaning with you, 3 = undecided/unknown, 4 = leaning against you, 5 definitely against you.) Keep tabs on all legislators, then add up the numbers in each category to gauge how you are doing. Focus your lobbying on the 2's, 3's and 4's.

- *Keep track of developments:* Lobbying is usually a constantly evolving process right up until the final vote is cast. It s not a one time event where you make your voice heard and then go home. Winning requires consistent follow up. As you and your allies lobby the same target list, information will be coming from every direction if everyone is doing their job. Of course, legislators have been known to tell one person one story and another person a different story, (imagine!), so targets will move up and down the scale depending on the most up-to-date intelligence. You have to keep all this straight to gauge where you stand and whether you might consider compromising if you think you will lose. Consider using a notebook (or a computer spreadsheet) with one page for each target.

Key Information for Tracking Officials

- *Who made the contact with the elected official*
- *When it was made*
- *What the official said about his/her position*
- *How they rated on the scale of 1 to 5*

Visit my website at DrewMcKissick.com ~ Connect on Twitter @DrewMcKissick

Armed with this information, you will begin to get a feel for which arguments are working and which aren't, and what objections need to be overcome. Remember, the argument that *you* may feel is the most persuasive may not be the same one that *they* feel is the most persuasive. You have to meet them on their own terms.

Use the latest intelligence to your advantage. The information you gather is only as good as the degree that you put it to use, so maintain close coordination with your coalition partners.

Since maintaining multiple lists will only breed confusion, one person should be designated to keep the master target list, (a "List Coordinator"). All information should then be passed through them. In the thick of the fight, such as the days leading up to a crucial vote, the coordinator should be touching base with coalition partners on a regular basis. Most of them can't be at city hall or the state capitol all the time, so pick a list coordinator who is close to the action, (such as a legislative staffer or even a legislator). Their job is to tell everyone else when to weigh in and who to target.

As General George Patton once said, "Information is like eggs; the fresher the better". When it comes to lobbying, the "fresher" your information, the better the odds that you'll be successful.

"Grasstops" Lobbying

...people who matter to those who matter

While the term "grassroots" means the average citizen, the term "grasstops" means community leaders. If you can match a local organization's grassroots with a similar network of grasstops leaders, you will see a tremendous leap in the ability to influence legislators. Grasstops is effective for many reasons. While many legislators may deceive themselves into thinking they can ignore or fool the average constituent, they don't usually feel the same about "Mr. Big" – and they don't want to get on his bad side.

Also, legislators can become insulated from grassroots pressure, part by design and part by choice. While many legislators don't like being bombarded by letters, they may choose not to read them. But they can't afford not to take a phone call from the president of the largest employer in the district. Similarly, the number of phone calls coming into a legislator's office eventually becomes irrelevant. All that registers in their minds is that they got a lot of phone calls. However, several calls from key community leaders will stick out in their minds.

Some Examples of Community Leaders

- *Pastors*
- *Large employers*
- *Other elected officials*
- *Party leaders*
- *Major contributors to the elected official*
- *Civic organization leaders*
- *Newspaper publishers*
- *Neighbors, relatives or friends (of the elected official)*

Some of these grasstops prospects may be "strange bedfellows". That's even better. The rule of thumb is: who do you know who can get directly to the legislator, not the staff? Whose phone calls have to get returned? Identify those people and approach them about joining your efforts. Keep a running list of them, (and who they can potentially influence), for future reference.

Cultivating Relationships

...win friends and influence people!

Remember, politics is all about people; people interacting and reacting to other people. How that happens usually comes down to what kind of relationships they have with one another. Bottom line? Build relationships. If you don't know your elected officials on a first name basis, then you need to. Make it a goal. If you don't think that they would return your call, then make that a goal too. Keep the following in mind as you try to establish relationships with public officials:

- *Have a strong local grassroots organization:* Become "Mr. Big" yourself by building an organization that gets noticed.

- *They want to know you:* Some people are intimidated at the very thought of meeting with a public official. Don't be. Look at it from their perspective. If you represent a strong local organization, they have a vested interest in knowing you. They know they can't have direct contact with all of their constituents, so they settle for their proxies – people who can reach other people. This means you.

- ***Contact them frequently:*** You're not likely to have influence with someone you don't know very well. So seek out opportunities to meet with them (socially or formally) and get to know them. Start with your own organization. Invite them to speak to your organization and turn out a big crowd. Book appointments to meet and lobby them on important issues. Do it all on a regular basis. <u>The more often they see you, the more of an impression you make.</u> Also, you should put aside the notion that you shouldn't touch base with them too often, (but don't be a pest either). Are they on Facebook, Twitter, or other social networking sites? Add them as a "friend" or "follow" them on those services.

- ***Be nice:*** There are plenty of people who have a lot influence with their legislators that is disproportionate to the clout they would otherwise seem to have. <u>That's because they made it a goal to see their legislators frequently, and then made it a goal to create a favorable impression.</u> You can be firm in support of your principles, but be nice. You want them to like you, not just put up with you.

- ***Don't avoid legislators who disagree with you:*** It's natural to only want to see our "friends", but when it comes down to crunch time <u>it's important to know the officials who are usually the "swing votes" on a target.</u> And don't forget those who hardly ever agree with you. Even they have a vested interest in knowing you. They don't want to incite you to oppose them when you may disagree. This is true even if it's unlikely that they'll return your phone call. <u>Just the fact that they know you called and asked for them personally sends a strong message that you're watching them.</u>

Prepare Your Message

...think before you speak

Once you've gathered all the relevant information, distill your concerns down into written talking points. This will help you and your allies think through the process and focus your arguments. Also, having written talking points will help you internalize and reinforce your position so that you can effectively articulate it when the time comes.

MAKE IT SHORT

If you can't get your message across quickly, then you haven't finished refining it. Go back to the drawing board. Find and highlight the most important points. Define consequences of action or inaction and use vivid analogies and examples. If it takes forever to follow an argument, then you've lost it. And remember, legislative offices are flooded with paper, and they throw most of it

11

away. <u>Letters and fact sheets should be no more than one page in length.</u> If a study or policy brief is more than ten pages, it should contain an executive summary of no more than one page.

PERSONALIZE THE MESSAGE

Theoretical and abstract arguments are not as good as explaining how an issue impacts real people's lives. Do research to find victims as well as success stories. A victim is a "poster child" who dramatically illustrates the problems with the policy you want changed, and a success story would be a "poster child" that illustrates the good things that will happen if your policy position becomes law. <u>Communicate something that people can easily identify with or relate to.</u>

KNOW THE OPPOSITION'S ARGUMENTS

If you understand what your opponents are saying, you will be in a better position to counter their arguments. Listening to those with an opposing view can often give you a perspective on an issue that you may have overlooked. Discuss the issue with a politician or an activist on the other side. Find out what they're thinking. <u>While you personally may not agree with their views, your challenge is to gain insight into all aspects of the issue so you can build a winning message.</u> Just remember to always be polite and courteous, yet firm in your beliefs. Then take what you've learned into account when finalizing your own message.

The Legislative Process

...making the sausage

Legislating is a messy business. As Otto Von Bismarck said, "Laws are like sausages, it is better not to see them being made". Virtually all legislation begins with a process of discussion, debates, and written drafts. At the local, state and national levels each bill or proposal has a procedure that it undergoes before passage, and each level is unique.

The status of each bill or proposal may have an impact on how you prepare and communicate your message. *<u>It is important to keep in mind that your message must be sharply focused so that all audiences have a clear understanding of what it is you seek to do.</u>*

Take note of the following areas where you and your local efforts can effectively influence legislation at the local, state and national levels.

COMMITTEES

Most work on legislation is done in committees, and this is often the best time to influence a bill. Public hearings begin here, changes are made, and delays or even defeats are possible. At the state and national levels, committee chairmen are key players at this stage, since they have the power to determine whether to consider the legislation, direct it to a subcommittee or possibly appoint a special study group. They can also be instrumental in influencing other committee members who are key to passage or defeat. As a grassroots activist, you can have an impact at this stage by personally contacting these officials with persuasive arguments for or against the legislation. In addition, you can attend meetings on the proposal and speak out to help shape public opinion.

LEGISLATIVE CALENDAR

Once favorably recommended by a committee, a bill is scheduled by legislative leaders (usually by the Rules Committee) for floor debate by the entire House or Senate, (locally the city/county attorney's office will usually pass the proposal to the council). Your involvement at this point could include contacting the key decisions makers, such as the Speaker of the House, Senate President Pro Tempore, Rules Committee members, council members, or legislative aides involved in these decisions, depending on what elected body you're focusing on. Focus on the people controlling the legislation.

FLOOR VOTE

This can come at any time after committee action and in one or both houses. At these critical points, all members decide a bill's fate, usually by a recorded vote. Most states allow amendments during this process. Seek out and work closely with other groups who share your values to ensure that legislators are contacted by as many like-minded activists and supporters as possible. If one chamber passes a bill, it must go to the other body for approval. If the second chamber passes the bill in the exact form, it then goes directly to the governor (or president) for signature. At the local level, passage by an entire council or board is usually the end of the process.

EXECUTIVE ACTION

Usually the chief executive, (president, governor or mayor), is required to take action by a certain time (either with a signature or a veto) or the bill automatically becomes law. Some states allow a "line-item veto," which enables some provisions to be vetoed without killing the entire bill. If the bill is vetoed, the legislature may attempt to override. Although rare, a strong expression of support or opposition at this point can help a governor decide whether to sign or veto a bill. A veto override will require a supermajority (usually two-thirds of both chambers of the legislative body). Usually it is too late to have an impact at this

13

stage. Before undertaking such an effort, carefully study your chances of victory and weigh them against the cost in terms of money and human resources.

If you need more information about the legislative process in general, and the differences at the federal, state and local levels, it is described in greater detail in Level Two of this series.

When Do You Compromise?

...when to hold 'em, when to fold 'em

Nobody likes to compromise – especially in politics. And when to compromise is always a difficult decision, given that individual circumstances will vary. Generally, compromise should be a last resort, (otherwise, what are you in this for?). After you have tried everything else, and you are convinced nothing else will work, then consider a compromise.

Tips on Compromise

- *Compromise if it is all you can get for now, and if it can lead to more victories down the road*

- *Compromise, if it is all you can get for now, and all you will ever get for the foreseeable future*

- *Do not compromise if getting "half a loaf" now hurts your chances to get the rest later*

- *Do not compromise on principle*

- *Ask for the bold version first – more than you think is possible – so you can compromise away some "bargaining chips" later if necessary*

14

Saying Thank-you

…"and I would like to thank…"

Everyone loves to be thanked, and politicians are no different. In fact, for most of them, it's a nice break from only hearing people complain.

Awards are a great low-cost / high-return way to say thanks to elected officials that have been helpful. And politicians love awards; which means that they're excellent tools for building relationships and rewarding deserving legislators. Awards can be subjective, based on leadership on a particular issue, (such as "Legislator of the Year"). If the award is objective, it should be based on a set of votes that you select, such as with a legislative scorecard that you might publish or votes you've tracked privately. This type of award can help your lobbying efforts as well. You can send out a "key vote notice" to legislators before they vote, letting them know that an upcoming vote is eligible for inclusion in your "scored" set of votes. (It lets them know people are watching)

Be if you do give out awards, be sure to send out a press release when any awards are given. The legislator's press secretary (if any) would *love* to work with you on this.

Advanced Lobbying Review

- *Do you need to fight?*
- *Can you win?*
- *Do your research.*
- *Consider forming a coalition with others.*
- *Get some high-profile ("grasstops") help.*
- *Cultivate friendships with elected officials.*
- *Prepare your message.*
- *Know the legislative process and plan strategy accordingly.*
- *Know when to compromise.*
- *Take the time to thank those who helped.*

Visit my website at DrewMcKissick.com ~ Connect on Twitter @DrewMcKissick

SECTION 2: CAMPAIGNS AND ELECTIONS

*"Bad officials are elected by good citizens
who do not vote." – George Nathan*

It's a fundamental truth of politics that if you don't win, you can't govern. You can't implement policy if you aren't elected to a position that allows you to do so, or if you don't have sympathetic elected officials that are willing to help. That being the case, it's critical that conservatives know the basics of effective campaigning.

Julius Caesar once said that the only thing needed to conquer the world was "men and money". Modify that idea slightly by adding "message" and you've got a good thumbnail sketch of what campaigns are all about.

The Three Fundamentals of Political Campaigns

- *Message: What are you saying?*
- *Money: Can you afford to get your message out to lots of people?*
- *Manpower: Do you have an organization to help you spread the word?*

These three principal elements are universal to all campaigns. They don't change. Regardless of whether the campaign is national, state or local in scope, the objective is the same. To win. And having the most compelling message, the most money, and the most devoted and numerous volunteers goes a long way towards that goal.

Visit my website at DrewMcKissick.com ~ Connect on Twitter @DrewMcKissick

Message

...what are you saying?

Message is all about what the campaign is saying. Why is the candidate running (or why is the issue on the ballot)? What is the campaign's vision and principles? A campaign's message should give voters a compelling reason to vote a certain way, based on things that are easy to understand and that they can identify with. It should be grounded in the values and concerns that voters already have. It should also be developed in accordance with the campaign's overall strategy, taking into consideration such things as partisanship, key issues as well as the images (or lack thereof) that voters have of the candidates. Finally, it should be repeated – over and over, and in multiple outlets.

THINK LOCAL

Local issues can move voters. Most people love to express their opinions on everything from foreign policy to balancing the federal budget, but these are issues that rarely motivate voters. Sure, we are concerned if a foreign crisis has an impact on our nation, especially if it means endangering American lives. We are concerned when the national debt may be a trillion dollars more next year. But the impact of a proposed local property tax hike, or a deep pothole on the road that you travel everyday, is more tangible and immediate than most national issues. It's a simple fact that people are more sensitive to issues that affect them every day in their own communities. So find a local focus. It will pay more political dividends to your cause.

TYPES OF MEDIA

How will you deliver your message? There are three basic ways in which a campaign can get its message out to the voters: "earned media", "paid media" and more recently, "social media".

- **Earned Media:** "Earned" means just that, you work for it. For every campaign (especially those at lower levels) this is critical. From press releases, op-ed columns, letters-to-the-editor, interviews, press conferences, events, etc., it all comes into play. This is where the information in the upcoming "Communications" section comes into play.

- **Paid Media:** Paid media is what it sounds like. It costs money. But it can be a powerful tool to get a campaign's message out. Paid media gives a campaign flexibility in crafting its image because it can be used to repeat the message and attempt to override low name identification or any negative publicity. Expensive but effective, it comes in many forms: radio and television ads, direct mail, the Internet (web banners, rented email lists), newspapers, magazines and billboards. Direct mail is called the

17

<u>"rifle-shot" approach to campaign messaging</u> because it can be tailored to individual demographic and geographic groups and target their specific concerns. <u>The same holds true for email</u>, provided you have a good database of email addresses and "know something" about the people on the list that determines what message you would send, or web-banner campaigns where you know the demographics of the people who regularly visit the sites you advertise on. Google's Adwords offers an increasing array of options, from targeted ad-words, web-banners on targeted sites (by category and location) to "do-it-yourself" radio and television ad placement, (SpotRunner also does TV ad production and buys online). In most lower-level campaigns, you shouldn't focus so much on paid media that you ignore the other (free) types of media, as well as putting together a good grassroots organization. View it as an "accessory", not a necessity.

- *Social Media:* This is a far newer phenomenon, but definitely not one to be overlooked. <u>Every campaign should have a strategy that makes sure they're visible on the various social networking platforms that people (read: voters) use.</u> What's more, these outlets make it easier for supporters you already have there to "recommend" your campaign to friends who may also be using those services, (helping you expand your presence "virally"). Services such as Facebook, MySpace, YouTube, Flickr, Twitter, etc., offer campaigns a means to expose themselves to people in yet another medium (reinforcing message), but also to engage those individuals, possibly pull them into the campaign's website and, hopefully "convert" them into supporters and/or donors. Social networks make it easier for your group to interact with people in the same way that they already interact with one another

These are all just channels for the message however. The important thing is the effectiveness of the message itself. And to judge that, ask the following questions:

Key Questions about Message

- *Is it compelling?*
- *Is it easy to grasp and identify with?*
- *Is it relevant to people's lives?*
- *Does it fit the voter's values?*
- *Is it repeated, and in multiple channels?,*
  (Repetition = Penetration = Impact)

Again, make sure that you review the "Communications" section of this manual for more thoughts about *"how"* to get your message out.

Money

...the mother's milk

The old saying that "money is the mother's milk of politics" is true. Money is the fuel that helps move the political machine. Money finances the campaign's communications (the "message") as well as its organizational efforts (the "manpower"). Those campaign ads and staff members don't pay for themselves.

Typically, the single biggest problem for any campaign is money. There's never enough. Just as every campaign wishes it had more time, they all wish they had more money. And to have money, (unless the candidate is independently wealthy), they have to raise money...which means asking for it. If you don't ask, you don't get it. The more people you ask – and the more who do the asking – the more the campaign will raise. And there are many ways to ask.

WHERE THE MONEY COMES FROM:

- *Personal Solicitations:* Most money is raised by the candidate asking for it personally, (and they all hate doing it).

- *Major donors / Finance committee:* This is a group of people who have agreed to raise or contribute a specific amount of money to the campaign – and are then held accountable to that amount.

- *Events:* This includes everything from receptions where guests give $500 a couple to meet VIP's, to neighborhood B-B-Q's where the food is donated and the cost is $15 a person.

- *Political action committees:* PAC's exist solely to give money to political campaigns, so take a common sense approach that targets those most likely to give to yours. You can find lists of PAC's and who they've given to here and here.

- *Party sources:* Assuming your campaign has won its party's nomination (if applicable), be sure to touch base with party leaders and attempt to include them in fundraising efforts.

- *Direct mail:* No doubt you've received multiple appeals in the mail from campaigns asking for money in the past. Most funds raised through this method are small dollar contributions ($50 or less).

19

- ***The Internet:*** Just as it's changed so much else, the Internet (via web sites, email and social networks) makes it possible to leverage the personal networks of pre-existing supporters and enlist them in online fundraising efforts, as well as reach people that are less connected to normal political and fundraising channels. <u>As Internet use grows, so will the importance of Internet fundraising.</u>

BUDGETING

It's one thing to have money, but it's another to manage it effectively. And campaigns are usually about the worst examples of prudent money management. Often they spend money as fast, if not faster, than they take it in. Just as with everything else, planning is the key and, when it comes to finance, that means a budget. <u>A campaign budget, or lack thereof, tells you everything about the campaign's priorities and whether the campaign is efficient and organized.</u>

<u>The campaign budget should be developed by its key leadership</u>, which typically includes the candidate, the campaign chairman, the campaign manager, the treasurer, and the finance chairman. The budget is really a projection of cash flow needs at various points during the campaign. <u>It does little good to plan campaign projects if the money isn't there to finance them when the time comes.</u>

Key Questions about Campaign Finance

- *Can the campaign raise the money it needs to communicate and organize?*
- *Is the candidate willing to ask for money?*
- *Does the campaign have a systematic, disciplined fundraising operation?*
- *Is the campaign efficient with the money that it raises?*

A campaign's budget can typically be broken down into two broad categories: *"voter contact"* and *"non-voter contact"* costs. *"Voter contact"* costs represents money spent trying to directly win the votes of individual citizens, (such as "paid media"). *"Non-voter contact"* costs represents money spent to support the campaign's efforts, but not directly on spreading the message. Below is an example of the typical breakdown in campaign costs.

20

Campaign Costs

Voter contact items include:

- *Television advertising, (broadcast and cable)*
- *Radio advertising*
- *Direct mail to voters*
- *Newspaper and magazine ads*
- *Billboards*
- *Paid telephone banks*
- *Web site*
- *Web banner ads / rented email*

Non-voter contact items include:

- *Salaries for staff and consultants*
- *Office space*
- *Office equipment and supplies (computers, copiers, printers, faxes, desks, chairs, etc.)*
- *Telephones and telephone lines for the office*
- *Staff expenses (mileage, lodging, meals, etc.)*

Look at how a campaign spends its money. The vast majority of the money spent on a well-run campaign will go to the "voter contact" projects like those listed above, (which means beware of any campaign that spends most of its money of "non-voter contact" items). When judging how well a campaign is doing in the finance department, answering the following questions will serve as good criteria.

Visit my website at DrewMcKissick.com ~ Connect on Twitter @DrewMcKissick

Manpower

...many hands = light work

A large group of supporters without any structure isn't an organization, it's a mob. Organization is about management, and the structure that makes management of the mob possible. Sun Tzu said that "management of many is the same as management of a few, it's just a matter of signals and banners" – meaning that, if all of the smaller elements of your campaign are organized properly, its larger elements will be as well. And it will be able to act and react when necessary.

A well organized campaign will have clearly defined lines of authority; meaning everyone knows who's in charge of what and who answer's to whom. In other words, it demonstrates who is taking care of each job that the overall campaign plan calls for. It should also be reflective of the campaign's resources. For example, you don't assign someone to handle putting out flyers if you don't plan to have the money to print the flyers.

With that in mind, an organizational structure should be put together *after* you've decided what resources the campaign will have and how it will use them. The rest of this section offers a breakdown of the typical campaign organization.

THE CANDIDATE

Campaigns are all about the candidate. Their name is on the ballot, so they run the show. But "how" they run it makes all the difference. A candidate's job should be threefold:

- *First, win votes* by getting in front of as many voters as possible – both in person and through the media.

- *Second, raise money.* The candidate should be the best fund-raiser for their own cause, (and people are more likely to respond to a personal appeal from the candidate themselves than from a proxy).

- *Third, make the final decisions*. Again, it's their name on the ballot. While candidates shouldn't run their own campaigns, they should make the final call on major decisions once they have considered the advice of the campaign committee, staff and/or any consultants.

A candidate should never plan and conduct his own campaign. The demands of actually "being" the candidate will prevent them from devoting the time necessary for planning and organization activities. Of course, if your "campaign" is a ballot measure or you're lobbying as issue, then you have no candidate and these responsibilities should be taken on by a "campaign committee" made up of all the principle players.

THE CAMPAIGN MANAGER

There's little use in having a plan unless it's being carried out. And that's where the campaign manager comes in. Their primary responsibility is to help plan the campaign's overall strategy (along with the other senior members of the campaign) and then to implement and execute the strategy. This means managing the campaign's day to day activities, such as dealing with staff and volunteers, making sure the campaign is staying on message and on budget, working to make life easy on the candidate, handling the unanticipated events which always arise and then making adjustments to the strategy as necessary.

Campaign Managers Should Be:

- *Skilled in the managing other people*
- *Willing to put in long hours*
- *Able to handle pressure and deal with emergencies decisively*
- *Objective*
- *Resourceful*
- *Trustworthy*

This is not a job for people with big egos. Campaign managers should be comfortable with working behind the scenes and out of the spotlight. A good rule of thumb is that their names should rarely appear in the newspaper in connection with the campaign. The campaign is about the candidate. And that's where the publicity belongs.

FINANCE COMMITTEE

Next to the campaign manager, the most important person in the campaign is the finance chairman. This is a person that agrees to take on the job of finding and raising the money needed to fund the campaign. As with everything else, in order to be efficient, you get organized. In this case, that means the Finance Chairman should oversee the organization of a Finance Committee – a group of people that come together and pledge to raise specific amounts of

23

money for the campaign, and are then held accountable to one another. It should be a broad based group, with representation from each geographic area and major business category in the district. Review the previous section on "money" to understand the various types of campaign fundraising.

GRASSROOTS STRUCTURE

In order to be effective, campaigns need organizational structure at the grassroots level which extends into the neighborhoods where people live and work. In campaigns for elected office, the "neighborhoods" are the precincts, as every election district in America is organized around them. This means that the organizational goal is to identify "captains" (coordinators) and volunteers in every precinct in the district. <u>Doing so should be the job of a grassroots committee chaired by a "Field Director".</u>

A healthy precinct-based grassroots network can become the backbone of a campaign in that it can ultimately "feed" all of the other volunteer efforts listed in this section. From doing neighborhood walks, to manning phone banks, to church outreach and getting out the vote on election day, it all takes people willing to do the work. <u>And the "grassroots" is where you find them and then organize them.</u> These are precisely the same reasons why political parties are organized in the same fashion. (If you need more information about how to organize at the local level, you should go back and review "Level 1" in this series)

VOLUNTEER COORDINATOR

Since most campaigns can only afford limited paid staff, the effective use of volunteers is critical. And that is why the selection of a good (if possible, experienced) volunteer coordinator can give most campaigns such a tremendous boost. They should be someone who is organized, patient and a "people person", non-egotistical – who knows how to mange the egos of others. <u>Someone who knows how to recruit, motivate and maintain the efficiency of volunteers is worth their weight in gold to any campaign.</u>

Generally, a volunteer coordinator is responsible for the following areas:

- *Recruiting others:* The first responsibility is to recruit enough qualified volunteers to do all the jobs needed by the campaign. Some volunteers will just show up at the headquarters, some will be recruited from local political clubs, and some have to be recruited from the friends and family of the candidate and others connected with the campaign.

- *Scheduling:* Determining who will do what, when and how and by when. They should maintain a master list of all volunteers, with full contact information and the areas they're willing to volunteer in (and which they may be best in). Then a schedule can be developed in accordance with the campaigns main calendar of activities.

- *Training:* The volunteers' chairman is responsible for training the headquarters' volunteers on greeting visitors, answering the telephone, filing, picking up the mail, and all of the other details handled by the headquarters staff.

- *Supervision:* Remember, every volunteer is at least worth what you pay them. Some are worth a lot more than others. Some come to work and some for social time, which means they need supervision.

The volunteers' chairman should also be alert to possible volunteers who could also serve as precinct captains or church contacts in other areas of the organization, (as discussed in volumes one and two of this series). These are positions that are critical to the "grassroots" nature of any political organization.

RESEARCH AND TARGETING COMMITTEE

If you don't know where you are, you can't get to where you want to be. That applies especially to politics because campaigns don't begin at square one and proceed in an orderly fashion. Basic research on the issues, values, voting trends, population, and general habits of the area where the election will be held is a must. For example, if two-thirds of the people in the area are senior citizens, it makes little sense to focus the campaign's message on issues that would appeal only to younger voters. As a result of this work, the committee helps prepare raw material for the campaign's communications.

Before you begin any attempts at organization you should make an effort to get to know as much as possible about the area you wish to organize. The Research Committee should obtain the current voter registration figures as well as the results of the past two general elections for all precincts in the district. (You can usually get this information from the county voter registrar's office or election commission, depending on the area you live in.) They should also obtain a map which identifies each precinct's geographic boundaries, (which you should be able to get from the same place as the election information, or at least find out where you should look). Ideally, you will want a map of precinct boundaries with a street map overlaid on top.

Given the limited resources that are usually available for political organization, it is important to focus your time, resources and volunteers where they will do the most good. In the world of political organization the process of identifying priorities is known as "targeting". It involves comparisons of past voting behavior and levels of voter turnout. Where precincts are concerned, you will divide them into three categories: "Republican", "Democrat" and "swing". The basic rule is to identify and focus on precincts that have the most reliable track record of

25

Republican support. The exception is that you can make allowance for areas that might deliver good returns if voters there can be moved on the basis of direct appeals on conservative issues.

Being successful and effective in grassroots organizing is a lot like trying to be successful at duck hunting. <u>You need to hunt where the ducks are.</u> Targeting will make the organization more effective, and save enormous amounts of time, resources, and energy in the future. <u>Don't skimp on it!</u>

<u>They should also be charged with doing what is called "opposition research",</u> meaning they should compile a file that includes the opponent's voting record, excerpts from speeches – especially those that may be inconsistent with currently stated positions – and any other information that might be useful. In any contest, it is wise to know as much as possible about your opponent.

The size of research committees will vary depending upon the nature, size and scope of the campaign. The more local the campaign, the less research needs to be done. However, <u>good research is a necessity in every campaign</u>, as the information it provides forms the foundations and assumptions on which much of the campaign plan will rest.

COMMUNICATIONS COMMITTEE

The communications committee (and/or the Communications Director) is responsible for getting the campaign's "earned media". This means getting the candidate on as many television shows, radio shows and in as many newspaper & website articles as possible. It means writing and distributing press releases, op-eds, letters-to-the-editor, live feeds to radio stations, and the production of video for television stations. <u>Be sure to review the "Communications" section of this manual for tips that will make the public relations committee more effective.</u>

SPEAKERS COMMITTEE

Every campaign can benefit from a few more voices. The speakers committee is a group of third-party spokesmen that can speak on behalf of the campaign when needed. Throughout the campaign, you're likely to have more opportunities for the candidate to speak than he/she has hours in the day, (and you should be actively looking for those opportunities). As a result, you'll need the help of others to get the message out. That's where a speakers committee comes in. In addition to speaking engagements, they can be used to offer quotes in press releases, authoring op-ed columns or submitting letters-to-the-editor. <u>It should be composed of a diverse group of individuals from all backgrounds and all across the district, with varying specialties that can be called on.</u> As a result, some of their personal credibility rubs off on the campaign.

GET-OUT-THE-VOTE COMMITTEE

The GOTV committee is one of the most important elements of any campaign. The point of a GOTV effort is to identify favorable voters and make sure that they get to the polls on Election Day. <u>Without a good GOTV effort, everything else you've done will likely be a waste of time and effort.</u>

At the outset of the campaign, this committee's first job is to set up and man the campaign's phone bank operation. A current list of registered voters should be acquired so it can be broken out and distributed among those participating in the phone bank effort, (either working en mass at central locations with many phone lines, or working individually at home). You must keep in mind the "type" of election, (primary or general), and therefore which voters are likely to vote in it, (hint: those that have before). <u>This will keep you from wasting time on those not likely to turnout anyway.</u>

Once the phone bank is set up, they should begin calling voters with a set of questions that will determine whether the voter is likely to support your campaign. This is followed by surveys to identify which issues are important to which voters, (so the campaign can approach them accordingly), and then straight up "advocacy" calls asking for their support. Just prior to, and on, Election Day the committee should call identified favorable voters to inform them that their vote is crucial, to encourage them to actually vote, and, if necessary, offer assistance in getting them to the polls. <u>Many campaigns are won or lost based on the strength of this effort alone.</u>

In order to make phone bank planning easier, there is a simple formula you can use. Take the total number of voters you wish to reach and divide by 1.7 (avg. # of voters per household), then multiply that number by 60% (avg. #of "reachable" households). The result is the number of calls that you need to plan to make in the initial round. Divide that by the number of phone bank volunteers and you have the number of calls each of them needs to make, (the more volunteers, the fewer the calls for each).

27

Four Types of Campaign Phone Banks

1. ***Candidate ID calls:*** *Simple surveys asking how the person would vote if the election were held today. The goal is simple – to find out who is "for" the candidate, "undecided" or "against".*

2. ***Issue ID calls:*** *These calls survey voters on issues to help identify conservative voters, (finding out who is pro-life, against new tax increases, for Second Amendment rights, or perhaps some local issue). Compare issue responses with "candidate ID" responses to find potentially favorable voters that were listed as "undecided".*

3. ***Advocacy calls:*** *Calls that deliver the campaign's best message quickly and simply, and then* asks *for a person's vote. Focus on the "undecideds".*

4. ***Get-out-the-vote calls:*** *Just before the election, the campaign calls its known supporters to remind them of their commitment, and how important their vote is. It should also remind them of the date of the election, and ask if they need help getting to the polls.*

The GOTV committee should also be responsible for planning and conducting door-to-door canvassing throughout the district. When it comes to how people vote on Election Day, effective, one-on-one personal communications has a greater impact than most people think. Generally, if a voter tells someone, (especially someone they may know from their own area), that they will vote for a candidate, they usually will.

In the course of conducting phone banks and neighborhood canvassing, the GOTV committee should take care to identify people who may need to vote absentee, and then get them the necessary forms or information to do so. Then verify that they did, (so those votes can be "banked" and you don't worry about them anymore). Rules for voting by absentee vary from state to state, so check with your local board of elections.

28

BALLOT SECURITY

Many candidates run good campaigns but still lose. Sometimes this is due to dishonesty at the polls. From incompetence, to intimidation, to suppression, to outright theft, the number of bad things that can happen at the polling place is long – and a good ballot security program can help you avoid voter fraud and any unwanted post election actions such as recounts or legal challenges. The goal is to have at least one experienced person serving as a "watcher" at each precinct on Election Day. This committee may be made up of volunteers who have been involved in other aspects of the campaign and are free on Election Day, but the person in charge should be an experienced veteran that has been involved in ballot security. Old pros can often spot problems that others will miss.

LEGAL

Like it or not, everybody needs a lawyer. Campaigns aren't much different. The real job here is to have someone who can help keep you from getting into trouble with the law, particularly when it comes to filing the proper forms with the government for your campaign. As un-American as it sounds, our government is increasingly in the business of regulating politics, requiring varieties of forms in various jurisdictions that force you to report on your activities, fundraising and expenditures, (among other things). But don't' let this detour you, (that's what they want!). Just find some cheap (even volunteer!) legal help. It will save you from some potential headaches down the road.

SCHEDULING

Along with money, time is one of the most precious resources in any campaign. And everyone has the same amount. Getting the most out of the time you have available comes down to good scheduling. Just as you shouldn't neglect having someone coordinate fundraising, you also shouldn't do without a scheduler. Someone needs to be responsible for keeping track of a "master schedule", which includes those for the candidate, the headquarters' staff and volunteers, as well as any key dates on the local calendar. When creating an overall campaign schedule, it's best to start with Election Day and work backwards. This helps you build in enough time to allow for the creating, printing and dropping of direct mail, any TV and radio, email, phone banks, neighborhood yard-sign blitzes, etc.

CAMPAIGN HEADQUARTERS

Every campaign needs a place to call home. Staff and volunteers need a place to come and work, and the public needs a place to come to learn about the campaign. Vacant storefronts, (donated if possible), are good because they are convenient and highly visible. The office is usually staffed by a campaign secretary (or the volunteer coordinator).

29

In the end, a good campaign structure will reflect the campaign's resources. The higher level the campaign, the greater the resources and the more intricate the structure will be. In lower level (local) races, you can usually get by with less structure and let people do double-duty.

> ## Key Questions about Campaign Organization
>
> - *Does it have clearly defined lines of authority?*
> - *Does it reflect the campaign's likely resources?*
> - *Does it have enough talented and committed volunteers?*
> - *Is the campaign staff talented, professional, committed and aggressive?*

Planning

...fail to plan, plan to fail

Every campaign needs a plan. But just as the plan is important, so is the process itself. Or, as General Eisenhower said, "plans are useless, but planning in indispensable". Although this book is not intended to get down into the gross details, suffice it to say that if you have no plan, then you plan to fail.

Having a written plan forces you to go through the planning process. It forces you to think things through, weigh options and see potential opportunities and problems. And to get the most out of any planning process and develop the best plan, all the key players who will be involved in carrying the plan out should be a part of the discussion.

Lay out the three key elements of "message", "money" and "manpower" in this section. What should be done, when, how and by whom in each area? What impacts the campaign? What are its advantages and disadvantages? How can you make the most your likely resources? (If this is an election campaign, then you need to research the voting habits of the precincts in the election district.) The answers to these questions become your plan. Then create a timeline working from Election Day (or any other critical day) backwards, building in enough time to get the things done that need doing. <u>This becomes your campaign calendar.</u>

As the situation in any campaign is always subject to change (because you have opposition), no plan ever survives contact with the enemy. Things change. So your plan has to be flexible and able to adapt to circumstances. Which means the "planning" doesn't end with the first draft. It's an ongoing process. <u>So once a plan has been implemented, schedule regular meetings of all the key players and review the situation.</u> Have things changed? Does any element of the plan or the timeline need to be altered to deal with those changes?

Use the following five steps of campaign planning to keep things on track.

The Planning Process

- *Do your research.*
- *Develop a plan. Write it down.*
- *Implement the plan.*
- *Evaluate the plan. Make necessary adjustments.*
- *Repeat…*

Remember, at the root elections are all about simple math: addition, subtraction, multiplication and division (no higher math here!). It's all about getting to fifty percent plus one.

Campaigns and Elections Review

- ***Message:*** *Do you know what you want to say? How and when you will say it? Is everyone on message? Does it resonate? Is it penetrating?*

- ***Money:*** *Are you meeting the budget? Have enough to implement the plan?*

- ***Manpower:*** *Do you have a good organizational structure? Precinct organization? Good distribution of duties? All the critical functions covered? Who will do what, when, where and how?*

- ***Plan:*** *Do you have a written campaign plan?*

SECTION 3: COMMUNICATING THE MESSAGE

"The art of communication is the language of leadership."
– James Humes

Communications is one of the most critical elements of any campaign or lobbying organization. It's one thing to know what you want to get accomplished, and still another to organize effectively, but without good public communications it can all come to naught.

If your organization is going to work with the media it should be through an appointed communications director or spokesman, (so make sure they read this section!). This person is primarily responsible for writing press releases and coordinating interviews and the media aspects of any events. They should be the person that the press comes to know as being responsible for providing them with information for their stories about the organization's activities. They should be someone with good written and verbal communication skills and who likes dealing with people – including the press.

This section of the manual will deal with "earned media", (the "free" kind that you have to work for!).

Where to Begin?

...first things first

Communications directors (or spokesmen) will find that, once they become known, local media will depend on them for news about your group (or campaign) and its activities. Before the first press release is written however, it is extremely important that you do some homework.

- **_Learn_** about each newspaper, radio and television station, and news or political website or blog serving your area and make a complete list of them and their key personnel, (create a spreadsheet with their contact information, and that of the editors and reporters at each outlet). A list of media outlets in your area can be accessed here.

- **_Listen_** to each radio station in your area. Learn which stations are news oriented and which are not. Make a note of when each station airs its news programs and whether or not they are locally produced. If they are only reporting news from a syndicated source like the Associated Press or a television network, they will not be a good source to cover your group. Be sure to listen for any special bias concerning news about conservatives groups or issues.

- **_Watch_** each television news show in your area, (or you record to view them later). Make a note of the names of the news anchors for each station's news programs. Seek out reporters who cover religion and politics and to develop a relationship with them.

- **_Read_** the newspapers and key blogs and websites covering your area. Get a good feel for how they cover politics and what sort of bias they may have. Make it easier to keep up with them all by getting their RSS feeds and/or using Google Alert to have stories on certain topics emailed directly to you each day.

- **_Introduce yourself_** to the people at each media source that you will be communicating with. Be sure to include any local correspondents for larger papers or television networks. Ask them how you can best work with them to help them do their job when your organization has something to communicate. Personal _contact is invaluable_.

- **_Learn the deadlines._** If you are dealing with a weekly or bi-weekly newspaper, when does the paper want the story? If you are dealing with a daily newspaper, radio station or television station, what time do they need the story? Then get your story in before their deadlines. If you do not make the deadline, the story will not be used. Daily newspapers, radio and television stations generally like late morning to mid afternoon for press conferences. This gives the television stations time to get the story on their evening news casts. Radio stations will air the story, with a possible sound bite, during their afternoon drive time news. Newspaper reporters will have the story in time to get their stories ready for the morning edition. Remember, if you miss a deadline, it's yesterday's news.

- **_Always be friendly!_** Never argue with reporters or editors. The one who controls the airwaves and the printed page will always have the last word. If your story is not used, it may not be because of the "liberal press", but because your news was bumped by more important news of the day or because it really was not that newsworthy. Or it could just be because an editor or reporter made a mistake. It's OK to ask, just be nice about it.

Getting Publicity

...look at me!

Just about everything that your organization does can be made into a newsworthy item. Discretion may dictate that some meetings will not be open for press coverage, but most meetings and public events are newsworthy for the local press.

> ## Examples of Newsworthy Items
>
> - *All official, public meetings of your organization*
>
> - *Organization activities, such as voter registration drives, petition drives or voter guide distribution*
>
> - *Announcements concerning awards, (such as "Legislator of the Year")*
>
> - *Announcing that volunteers are needed for community projects*

By way of example, let's say your local group is planning a dinner with a recognizable guest speaker. While your event by itself may not be newsworthy, your guest speaker, or an announcement about a new public policy position by your organization, *is* newsworthy. Start early! The better course of action is to release details about the event a little at a time. Besides, if you try for the big splash, your news release could contain so much information that it will be difficult to report. Write a series of shorter press releases and stagger their distribution. From this one event, you should be able to prepare newsworthy press releases about each of the items that follow.

- Announce the dinner, the main speaker, and the name of the chairman putting together the dinner.

- Provide a picture and biography of the speaker.

- Provide more specific information about the dinner. Will there be a major announcement or will the main speaker say something that will generate news?

- Write a reminder story about the event.

- Write the "Dinner to be held tonight" story, recapping the details.

34

- Write a follow-up story about the dinner telling how many attended, including a summary of the speaker's remarks.

You would only want to attempt this much publicity for a large event. But you should be able to get several stories about even an average event if you use your imagination a little.

In addition to regular activities of your group (or campaign), you can also get publicity by working piggy-backing on a pre-existing story. In other words, take a hot issue that already IS news and then find an angle to work your group into the story, (such as putting out a press release to comment on it, staging a protest, launching a petition, etc.). The key it to get "into" the story before the story runs. So if it's happening today, contact the press today.

Working with the press

...caution: handle with care!

Everything in life comes with some basic rules and working with the press is no different. Below is a list of some basic ground rules you should always keep in mind when it comes to the media. Stick to them and you and the stories you push will be much better served.

- ***Have ONE news source for your group.*** Your name on the news release will become familiar quickly.

- ***Never use pressure or influence to try to get a story done.*** Reporters will resent it, (and you).

- ***Always treat members of competing news outlets equally.*** Don't play favorites or offer "scoops'. The editors and reporters will respect you for your fair dealing with them. Respect builds trust, which you will need as you deal with the press over the long haul.

- ***Cooperate with reporters.*** If one asks you for details on a story, answer his or her questions without attempting to be evasive. If you do not know the answers, find them and call the reporter back, making sure to first ask about their deadline.

- ***Don't make it a habit to talk to reporters "off the record".*** As a rule, if you don't want something reported, then keep it to yourself!

- ***Do not thank a reporter for doing a story.*** It's their responsibility to report your story because it's news, not because you asked them to. On

35

the other hand, it is perfectly acceptable to mention that a story was well done and fair, (everyone likes some praise now and then).

- ***Always be accurate!*** If you're not sure about information, don't pass it on. Be sure about names, dates and other details.

Press Releases

...shaping your own story

The purpose of a press release is to communicate news about your organization and to effectively get your message out to the public. That being the case, the first rule of writing one is to make sure that you have a well defined message that will benefit your group, campaign or issue. If you simply send out press releases in an attempt to attract publicity, you'll soon lose credibility and defeat the purpose of establishing good working relations with the media.

WRITING THE RELEASE

A press release should be written simply, clearly, and accurately. Editors don't have the time to correct your spelling, syntax or grammar, or wade through a lot of rhetoric to get to the facts – which is the only thing they're interested in.

News stories are written as inverted pyramids, which means you should take the same approach to writing your press release. The most important facts should be placed in the opening sentences, followed by an explanation and the story development. The least important material should be placed at the end. If the editor thinks the story is too long for the space available, he can edit it by removing the material at the end without damaging the important facts at the beginning. By writing the release in this way, you increase the chances that your story will appear in print, (as they'll have less editing to do). Some smaller outlets that have limited staff will often use your press release word for word if you follow these rules.

Most people look for local interest in news stories, so *the more local you can make your press release, the more likely the editor is to use it*. Also be careful not to load the story down with opinion or editorial comments. Keep it centered on who, what, when, where and why. Keep opinion limited to any attributed quotes you may use.

HEADLINES

You can suggest a headline for the editor by placing your own headline at the top of your press release. Which stories usually catch your interest? The answer is probably the stories with the best headlines. So be creative. If you are fair about the subject of your story, you can often influence the editor's thinking about how the final headline will read.

LEAD PARAGRAPH

The first paragraph is called the lead, and it's the heart of your press release. A good headline gets you in the door...but what will keep people interested and wanting to know more? That's where your lead paragraph comes in. It's your second chance to create a headline. Your goal is to tell the entire story in just a few sentences and as few words as possible. Write in a way that will make the editor and reader want to keep reading. *If the editor does not want to read any more, the reader will never see your story.* By answering the questions "who?", "what?", "when?", "where?", "how?" and "why?", your lead will be factual, clear, and in the proper news style. Always include the date of your press release in your lead. If you need examples, just review the articles in your local newspaper.

For example:

> ANYTOWN, January 1, 2008 - John Q. Citizen, chairman of the (your organization), today announced the appointment of Joe Blow as Director of (organization) Finance Committee.

> ANYTOWN, September 1, 2008 – John Q. Citizen, Chairman of the (organization), will speak on "Pro-family Politics and Activism" as the keynote speaker at a special dinner sponsored by (organization) at 7:30 p.m., Thursday, September 11, in the Grand Ballroom of the Hyatt Regency Hotel.

JUST THE FACTS, MAM

In any news story, your personal opinions don't count for anything! No matter how enthusiastic you are about your group or the issue at hand, you should restrict opinions to quotes you might use from official spokesmen. Don't write that "the audience was enthusiastic', just mention that the audience cheered and applauded – but only if they did. Don't write that "a large crowd attended the rally', as "large" is subjective. Instead, just report how many were in attendance. Include an animated quote from someone if possible, to give it a little more pizzazz, (the press loves a good quote).

LENGTH

The length of the release depends on its importance, meaning its importance to the public, (not you). Your story may be told in two or three paragraphs, while others may require a second page. <u>Editors like short, concise stories best.</u> If they want more, they will usually ask for it. Give the media all the important facts, and let the editors decide how much to use. <u>Remember, the less verbiage you offer, the more likely they are to use what you do offer, (if they actually do the story of course).</u>

FORMATTING

Remember, reporters and editors are busy people who are driven by daily deadlines. The easier you make their job, the more likely they will run with your story. And the better your release is formatted, the less work they'll have to do – and the less likely they'll take a pass on it. <u>With that in mind, here are some general formatting guidelines you should consider.</u>

- Use at least one inch margins and double spaced text.

- Type your name, address and phone number in the upper left corner as the contact person, so you can be reached quickly if the editor has any questions.

- Under the contact info, add the "release line" in capital letters, (such as "FOR IMMEDIATE RELEASE" or, for a specific date and time, "FOR RELEASE THURSDAY, 3:30 PM, APRIL 12, 2009")

- Give it a good headline (in capital letters, centered over the body text).

- Start the story about one-third of the way down the page to allow the editor sufficient space for editorial instructions and headlines. Remember, the first paragraph is the most important, (containing the all important "who", "what", "when", "where", "how" and "why" details). The following paragraphs then build on that, providing more details and/or quotes you want to add.

- Indent each paragraph.

- Limit it to one page. If it is longer than one page, type "MORE" (centered) at the bottom of the first page and then number all other pages. Generally, your releases should never be longer than two pages.

- Don't break paragraphs between pages, if possible.

- After the final paragraph, type "###" or "-30-" to signify the end, (don't ask why, just do it!).

38

TIMING

Events occurring today must be reported today, either by telephoning the story to the editor or by writing and delivering it immediately. <u>Two days later is too late.</u> Ask editors and reporters which days are usually busy news days and which are light days. Generally, the first part of the week provides the best opportunity to get your message out. And when Congress is out of session, news outlets often look for local stories dealing with how grassroots activists lobby their representatives while at home.

PHOTOGRAPHS

Newspapers are always looking for good pictures to help tell the story and give the paper more visual appeal. If your organization is planning an event with good photo possibilities, call and suggest that the editor might want to send a photographer to cover it. Be sure to call the editor well in advance of the event to give him time to schedule a staff photographer. If the editor asks you to send pictures instead, (which may happen with some small newspapers), get your own photographer or do it yourself. Keep each photo simple, no more than four people in each picture. <u>Do not use posed pictures.</u> Have the subjects do something, such as look at an award, shift through a bunch of papers, move something, or even be speaking. Posed pictures are dull! <u>Photos should be taken with a digital camera</u> so you can then email them to the editor along with a note identifying each person in the picture, (left to right), and describe what they are doing.

DISTRIBUTION

See the section on "Delivering your message" at the end of this chapter.

> **REMEMBER:** *People rarely care about what you do as much as you do, so you have to work to get their attention and keep them interested.*

Managing Event Coverage

...keeping their eye on the ball

When an important meeting or a large event is coming up, (one that might deserve press coverage), invite the press well in advance. The following outline will help you organize your contacts with the press:

BEFORE AN EVENT:

- *The memorandum:* About a week ahead, fax or hand deliver a memo to editors and radio and TV news directors. Be sure to mark it "MEMORANDUM NOT FOR RELEASE" so they will know the information is background only. Briefly describe the coming event. What is going to happen? Who is going to speak? Will there be good visuals? Just give them the facts. Give them the day, date, time, and the place (be sure to give the street address). Include your name, address, and telephone number just as you would in a press release.

- *Follow-up:* A few days before the event, follow up with another memo-randum and a telephone call to editors as a reminder. Remember, you will be calling a newsroom that receives dozens of calls each day from various organizations that all want press coverage. Be brief in reminding them about your event. If you ask whether a news crew will be coming, don't be surprised if you don't get a commitment right then on the phone. Assignments for news coverage are usually made at the last minute.

- *Admission:* If admission is being charged for the event, *never* ask news people or photographers to pay. They are your guests. Be fully prepared for them and be ready to cooperate with them. However, the media may offer to pay for their own meals to reinforce their objectivity. So be prepared to let them if they ask.

- *Press Table:* Arrange to set up a press table equipped with all the prepared materials, (see "press packets" below), plus extra pens and paper. If the event is very large and many reporters will be attending, you may want to reserve a "press room" for reporters. This is a quiet room with more tables and electrical outlets so reporters can set up computers to write their stories or call their editors. If your budget permits, you might also add a refreshments table as well. Arrange for one of your most reliable supporters to staff the press area.

PRESS PACKETS

Well in advance, you should prepare press packets that contain the type of information listed below. Plan to have enough for all invited members of the media.

- *The speech:* When possible, obtain an advance copy of the speaker's speech and have it available for the press when they arrive, (or excerpts from it). The reason for this is to ensure that they have correct information to use in a story, and it also helps avoid being misquoted. Do not release this in advance of your event.

- *Bios:* Prepare (or obtain) a brief biography with background information about the speaker or any special guests. Also include a sheet with your organization's "about us" information.

- *Guest list:* Prepare a list of head table guests and any prominent people who are invited.

- *"Cover story":* A press release about the event written in a straightforward news style, in past tense, describing the event, who was there, what occurred, etc., (helps "shape" their coverage somewhat).

- *Handouts:* Include copies of any handouts you've created for the event, (such as fact sheets, issue backgrounders, etc.)

AT THE EVENT

Reporters are attending your event because it is their job to report the news, so have everything ready. Have someone at the door to greet and direct them to the press area and show them what's been made available for them. Invite them to meet people they can interview for stories, (especially those you have prepped for such interviews ahead of time). The cooperation you show the press and the information you give will pay off in the future.

> **REMEMBER:** *Always try to anticipate the media's needs for information. The more that you can "spoon feed" them, the better off you'll be.*

41

Giving Interviews

...you have the right to remain silent

This section will give you an overview on how to successfully deal with the media and get your message across to the public. Some of it is just plain common sense, but it's useful to review these points and keep them fresh in your mind, as it's easy to get distracted by the demands of the press.

APPEARANCE

How you look reflects on yourself and the group you represent. So it goes without saying, (but I'll say it anyway), you should always be well-groomed and neatly dressed for TV interviews. If you're sitting for the interview, your tailbone should be at the back of the chair. This will also help you breathe easier. You don't want to be taking obviously deep breaths, because it makes you look like you're uncomfortable with what you're saying. If you're wearing a suit coat, try and sit on the bottom back edge of it, so it doesn't rumple up on your shoulders on camera. Also, keep it unbuttoned and allow it to hang naturally. Maintain good posture at all times. <u>Lean forward slightly to show that you're confident and in control.</u> Leaning backward makes you look defensive. <u>If you are standing, plant your feet about shoulder width apart, with your weight evenly distributed.</u> You don't want to be shifting your weight from one foot to another during an interview, especially in front of a television camera. It makes it easier on the cameraman to keep you "in frame", and it keeps you from looking uncomfortable with the questions you're being asked.

BRIDGING

Bridging is the most important tool you will ever use in your dealings with the media. There will be times during an interview when you'll want to make a transition from a negative question to a positive point. The technique used to deal with these situations is called bridging. This is simply a way to get back on the message that you want to communicate. Don't avoid answering a negative question, just move through it quickly and confidently, and get back on your message. The worst thing you can do is avoid answering, as it makes you look evasive. *<u>The idea is to answer the question in the first few seconds and then "bridge" to your main message.</u>* This brings up another important point: *<u>always know what subject you're going to talk about and what message you want to get across BEFORE you do an interview.</u>*

Four Keys to Effective Bridging

1. ***Know what you DO want to talk about:*** *(Otherwise, what's the point?)*

2. ***Write down the question you least want to answer:*** *Once you have this in mind, think of a suitable "bridge" from it to something you do want to talk about.*

3. ***Write down the question you have the hardest time answering:*** *Once you have this down, give some thought to constructing the correct answer. Continue working on the answer until you're comfortable with it and it comes naturally. Read it out loud several times.*

4. ***Practice, practice, practice***

CONTROLLING AN INTERVIEW

When you give an interview, remember that you have certain rights which you should exercise before being interviewed. For example:

- ***The right to be prepared:*** Set the ground rules up front. Ask questions about the reporter and his publication or broadcast before you begin the interview. Ask them what kind of story they're doing and how they see you (or your group) fitting into it. If you're uncomfortable with the direction and scope of the story, tell them about your concerns. It's important to be able to have a clear understanding of the story and what type of questions you'll be asked. The more information you have, the more confidence you'll have during the interview. You should never be surprised by a reporter's question. If you're well prepared and you ask the proper questions before you go on the record, the interview should go well. In addition, it's also a good idea to find out who else is going to be interviewed for the story. For example, if groups that take a different position from yours will be part of the story as well, you can perhaps anticipate their response and use your interview to refute what they're likely to say, (or put them on the defensive).

- ***The right to be comfortable:*** If you're uncomfortable, it will come across in the interview and you'll potentially look unpleasant or defensive. Don't' stand with the sun in your eyes during an outside interview. On a TV set, make sure bright lights are not shining directly into your eyes. Don't frown or appear angry, but don't appear too jovial either. <u>Work to maintain a calm, confident yet pleasant demeanor.</u>

- ***The right to answer without interruption:*** Use your best judgment about objecting if you get interrupted, (you don't want to let it make you look angry or defensive). <u>You don't want to appear too sensitive, but you don't want to let yourself get bullied either.</u>

<u>The key is control of the interview.</u> You should be believable and natural, and you should exercise your rights to maintain control of what you want to say and how you say it. While you want to be sensitive to reporter's deadline pressures, you should never allow those pressures to compromise what you're trying to accomplish by doing the interview.

18 TIPS FOR BETTER INTERVIEWS

1. ***Never feel obligated to do an interview without notice.*** If a reporter calls you cold, find out the direction of the story and what issues will be covered. Tell them you will get back in touch as soon as possible, then take time to consult with your leadership (if any) or an advisor before offering comments.

2. ***Always ask about their deadline.*** Reporters work under tight schedules. If the information is needed before you think you can supply it, explain the situation, but do your best to help them.

3. ***Be informed.*** Know your topic and have supporting material to back it up.

4. ***Anticipate touchy questions.*** Have your answers ready and be prepared to "bridge".

5. ***Be fully briefed.*** About the reporter, the news organization, and the direction of the story.

6. ***Be comfortable.*** Interview in a setting you're comfortable with.

7. ***Maintain good eye contact***. Don't be distracted by the surroundings (or a camera).

8. ***Stay cordial.*** Even when they're not.

9. ***Answer questions directly.*** Offer your conclusion first, and then back it up. If you don't know the answer, say so and offer to get the answer. Then follow up.

10. ***Only answer one question at a time.*** If asked several questions at once, point that out and then respond to them individually.

11. ***Never answer hypothetical questions.*** Limit your comments to the specific issue that you want to address.

12. ***Never make off-the-record remarks.*** If you don't want it public, don't say it.

13. ***Don't automatically accept information presented by a reporter.*** Tell them that you're not familiar with that specific information, but would like to respond to the basic issue.

14. ***Never speak for others.*** If you're asked about the opinions or positions of an absent third party, such as a leader from another conservative group, say, "I can't speak for them, but our position is…"

15. ***Remember your audience.*** That means the general public.

16. ***Remember the lighting.*** When it comes to TV, black suits absorb too much light for the cameras. Dark blue or gray suits look better, and light blue shirts and blouses reflect less light than white ones.

17. ***Be available for follow-up.*** A reporter may need to ask a follow-up question or get a clarification after the interview. (Just make sure they don't use a follow-up to sandbag you!)

18. ***You're always "on".*** Don't assume that when a reporter stops taking notes or the camera stops running that the interview is over. Reporters also rely on their memories for information.

SPEAK WITH ONE VOICE

When using the media to communicate your message is important that you speak with one voice. Meaning that you should always consult with your leadership (if any), or other conservative groups or allies, and discuss key talking points and the message you want to deliver. Make sure that you're not sending conflicting messages, as this defeats the purpose of good communications.

Types of News Outlets

...~~don't~~ feed the animals

RADIO & TELEVISION

The easier you make things on local radio and TV outlets, the more likely you can get good coverage from them. If a camera crew is sent by a TV station to cover your event, help them find a good area to set up their equipment that offers a good view of the action. Give them a rundown on who's who at your event and a schedule of what's going to happen. Try and anticipate the needs of a sound crew when it comes to the positioning of microphones. Keep in mind that they're likely to want to do one-on-one interviews at some point. Know ahead of time "who" you want to have interviewed and make sure that they're fully prepared. Have a quiet place (even a room) set aside where interviews can be conducted without distractions. Also, when it comes to television, remember that it's a visual medium. People "watch" TV more than they listen to what's said. Think about your event in terms of visuals, because the TV crew certainly will. What visuals best portray the message you're trying to get across? Try to use them.

NEWSPAPERS

Keep in mind that newspapers come in all different varieties, (daily, weekly, tabloid, etc.), and each has a different focus and style. Make an effort to accommodate them. Remember, the smaller the paper, the more likely they are to run just about whatever you give them. Most of the basics you need to know concerning newspapers is covered in the previous section concerning press releases.

WIRE SERVICES

Wire services can help you broaden your coverage. Consult with the bureau chief of The Associated Press when you think your story may have more than just local news value. The wire service often uses releases of state and regional interest as well as national news stories. Sometimes these smaller interest stories can become national news, or at least be distributed regionally.

BLOGS AND WEBSITES

More and more Americans get their political news online each year. In fact, the 2008 election marked the first time that the more Americans got their news online than from print media; and at this rate, it will eclipse television news in the near future. So what does this mean to you? It means that you don't ignore the Internet as a news outlet. It means that you treat online news sources and political websites and blogs just as importantly as other more traditional outlets.

46

In many cases, these "new media" sources serve to influence how the old media reports a story, or even prompts them to break a story to begin with.

PUBLIC SERVICE ANNOUNCEMENTS

The public broadcast industry gives away millions of dollars worth of public service announcements (PSA's) each year, so be sure and consult with your local broadcast stations about their policies. These are free and are a good resource; however, broadcast time is limited and PSA's may be aired at times that fail to reach your audience. Use them when you can, but never rely on them to get your message across. Don't send a proposed PSA to station directors without first contacting them first. Let them know what you're interested in and ask if they have any advice. Then thank them for their help and abide by any conditions they lay out. In the end, you actually want your PSA to be aired, and that's up to them. So try and establish a good working relationship with them.

Suggested Communications Tactics

...tools of the trade

FACT SHEETS

You can't expect people to get the facts right about your message if you don't provide them. By preparing a fact sheet on any given issue, you can provide background information, point-by-point narratives, or answers to frequently asked questions and your conclusions. Also provide a list of contact names and information so those who may have questions can get in touch with them.

PRESS RELEASES

(AS DISCUSSED IN THE "PRESS RELEASES" SECTION)

PSA'S

Take advantage of the free publicity PSA's can offer. Write a 15 and/or 30 second PSA's (depending on length stations want) with concise and specific information on the topic you want addressed. Use key talking points from any fact sheets as a basis for the PSA format. Provide a name and contact information on the PSA so those who may be interested can follow up for more information or volunteer to help. Distribute it to all media outlets.

LETTERS TO THE EDITOR

Writing a letter to the editor of your local paper is not difficult, and can be more influential than you may think. Limit the letter to one subject and be brief. Keep it civil. List your concerns and articulate the facts. Don't base it on emotion, (it's not as effective as a letter based on fact). When preparing your message, work diligently to simplify it so that it can be easily understood by all who will read it. <u>Articulate and succinct views are always better appreciated.</u> Don't overlook smaller publications, such as weekly papers, magazines and local websites and blogs. Make sure you stay within any guidelines they may have for such letters or comments, (such as the number of words, supplying your contact information, etc.).

OP-ED COLUMNS

Op-eds (or guest commentary columns) are a great and inexpensive way of getting a message out and helping shape public opinion. You should make it a point to have a regular schedule of having someone from your group (or a respected person with your point of view) submitting guest op-eds to your local media.

A Good Op-ed can:

- *Raise the profile and credibility of your group*

- *Increase public awareness of important issues*

- *Mobilize public support*

Here are some quick tips to writing a great op-ed:

1. *Check the guidelines:* Most newspapers prefer op-ed pieces in the range of 600 to 800 words. Check with each media outlet for their submission guidelines. Get a sense of what their editors will be looking for by becoming familiar with the other op-eds they print every day. <u>Try to have an angle that the editor would appreciate</u>, (the more local the media outlet, the more local the focus should be).

2. *Be Timely:* Keep up with the news and look for opportunities to work a local news angle into your article. Timing is the key. <u>The more current and relevant to the topic, the better your chances of being published.</u>

3. *Stay focused:* Space is limited, so the fewer points you're trying to make the better. If you can't work your main point into one or two sentences, then you need to refine it. <u>Identify a few points that support your</u>

<u>argument and build the article around them.</u> Be clear about your position. Don't equivocate. Make an effort to anticipate and refute the arguments of your opposition.

4. ***Make your main points first:*** Get to the point quickly and convince the reader that it's worth their time to keep reading. Draw them in by making sure that the first paragraph catches their attention. <u>When writing an op-ed, you state the conclusion first.</u> Make your strongest point, and then spend the rest of the article supporting that point. Provide some initial background information, but don't let it overwhelm your article.

5. ***Explain why the reader should care:*** <u>Put yourself in the place of the reader looking at your article.</u> At the end of every few paragraphs, ask yourself: "so what?". Then answer the question. What will your suggestions accomplish? What should they mean to the reader? Offer specific recommendations. Look for great examples that illustrate your argument and use personal anecdotes and humor to draw the reader in. <u>Help educate them without being preachy.</u>

6. ***Don't be verbose:*** Use short sentences and paragraphs. <u>Your writing should be crisp, clear and to the point.</u> Look at the style in the papers (or websites) you wish to contribute to. They're writing to be read by the largest audience possible, not drown people in verbiage. Use active, not passive language.

7. ***Make your ending memorable:*** As mentioned, it's important to have a strong opening paragraph, but it's also important to close well. You want a short, strong closing paragraph that neatly, (and memorably) summarizes your argument, (perhaps even cleverly restating that point you made in the opening paragraph). <u>Restate your position and call people to action.</u>

8. ***Provide some "about you" information:*** Provide your standard contact information, as well as one or two sentences describing who you are, what you do, and any other information you think the editor should be aware of. For example: "John Q. Citizen is an Anytown, USA based political activist with Concerned Citizens". <u>Help them let everyone know who you are and what you're about.</u>

THIRD PARTY SPOKESMEN

When possible, identify and engage reputable individuals to speak on behalf of your efforts, (especially if you're in a campaign). Such individuals in effect lend their own credibility with the public to your efforts, (especially if they are viewed as experts in a field that relates to the subject you're working on). If possible, create a "Speakers Committee" of those who are available (and qualified) to speak on behalf of your efforts. <u>Not only will this lend more</u>

49

credibility, but it can help spread the work load and make the group more effective.

TARGET YOUR AUDIENCE

Your audience consists of the countless others who share your views and can form an aggregate voice large enough to influence decision makers. In other words, it can be greater than the sum of its parts, (and have more influence). Once your message is prepared, make a concerted effort to have it reproduced and delivered in many forms. Not everyone gets their information from the same source. Identify the audiences that will help generate the greatest response for what you're doing and target them. The general public receives information in many forms and from many sources, such as paid advertising, news media reports, free media and word of mouth. None of these avenues should be overlooked.

Don't forget to target the decision makers as well. If there are council members, board members, or congressmen who will be voting on the outcome of an issue, and they are undecided or opposed to your group's position, target them first. Identify media outlets and other interest groups that can help distribute information in their districts. Those who serve in positions of political power, such as committee chairmen and political party leaders, have lots of influence as well and should be approached accordingly. For example, although a city manager may not directly determine the outcome of a city council vote, the position he or she takes on the issue can be used to pressure those who will be voting on the issue.

DELIVER THE MESSAGE

By now you have prepared a message to be delivered in different forms through different channels. You've gathered your information, set your message and targeted your audience. Now keep the following guidelines in mind when distributing your message:

- ***Send your press release to key media outlets:*** It doesn't do you any good if nobody reads it! First, you should have a good database of all press contacts in your area that are likely to cover your issue. Make it as complete as possible with full contact information, (email addresses, phone & fax numbers and mailing addresses). Click here for a good resource to find your local media contact information and start building your database. Media outlets in the districts of your targeted elected officials should be prioritized. Television, radio, newspapers, local magazines and key news and political websites should all get copies. Email and/or fax would be the best methods for distribution. Also, if you have a website, you should be able to put it on your site and distribute your information via an RSS feed, in addition to having an email

50

subscription option for your press releases. There are also free services that will distribute releases to databases they have already put together, but they won't necessarily know which reporters are covering your "beat". Use at your own discretion.

- ***Send your PSA to radio and TV stations for immediate broadcast:*** Depending on your message, you may want to focus on more conservative outlets, such as Christian radio and TV and/or conservative talk radio.

- ***Distribute copies of fact sheets and op-eds (if any):*** These should be sent out to all key contacts in your organization. Church contacts can give the information to members of their church and civics concerns ministries. Precinct captains can distribute to their neighborhood volunteers, and any others can distribute to likeminded friends and family.

- ***Make the message available via email and social networks***: For best result, make it available in a format that people can easily forward on to others, (such as a pre-formatted, printable documents, like "Word" or "PDF" files), which people can easily print on a desktop printer and distribute to others. This is another reason why it's so important to identify the email addresses of your supporters, as well as work to identify conservative websites and bloggers that may cover politics in your area. Put them on your list as well. Encourage supporters to help spread the message via social networks like Facebook, MySpace, Digg, Delicious and Twitter. Get things rolling yourself if you have an account with these services.

- ***Distribute copies of "letters-to-the-editor":*** Send them to organization members and key contacts, and encourage them to write similar letters. If an editor begins to receive a lot of letters regarding a specific issue, he may decide it is an issue worth doing a story about.

- ***Maintain a website:*** You don't have to be a rocket scientist anymore to maintain a website, much less to be able to get your information out on the web in a way that people have quick and easy access to. You can buy internet domains for your group cheap via sites such as GoDaddy, and/or start a blog with service such as Blogger or Wordpress. This will then give you a central location to maintain your information and make it easily available to any supporters. From there, it's easy to add RSS feeds to your site (syndication of your content) which anyone can grab and consume in any number of ways, or to simply email out links to new an interesting items as you add them to your site. Maintaining a regular blog is a virtually cost-free way to control and defend your message and communicate it to an interested audience.

- Again, you can easily add a presence on social networking sites such as Facebook (create a "group"), and mini-blogs such as Twitter, or even pure online campaign sites such as AktNow. The point is that it's easy to share your information with literally everyone. Don't sell your message short.

Delivering an articulate, positive message is an ongoing process. Whether you win or lose in your current effort, you should continue to maintain good relations with key members of the press and leading policy makers. In a rapidly changing political environment, few issues are ever final. Maintaining these relationships allows you to be heard long before a measure reaches a critical stage. Often, just by expressing the conservative viewpoint, groups and individuals can help build momentum for the conservative movement in general.

In the end, "how" you communicate can be just as important as "what" you communicate. Don't let style overwhelm your message. And remember the old English proverb: "Use soft words and hard arguments".

Communications Review:

- ***Know what you want to say:*** *Get the message down before you speak.*

- ***Learn your media audience:*** *Do your homework. Who are they? What do they cover? Get their info.*

- ***Make news:*** *Do something newsworthy…or work into a pre-existing story.*

- ***"Help" the press:*** *Spoon feed them exactly what you want them to cover. Do their work!*

- ***"Package" your news:*** *Write a good press release to help steer coverage of your story.*

- ***Learn how to do an interview:*** *Know your rights. Learn how to "bridge"!*

- ***Speak with one voice:*** *Don't confuse the media (or the public) with multiple messages.*

- ***Target your audience:*** *Focus on those who want or need your message.*

- ***Deliver the message:*** *Saturate all available outlets.*

Visit my website at DrewMcKissick.com ~ Connect on Twitter @DrewMcKissick

SECTION 4: PARLIAMENTARY PROCEDURE

"If you don't know the rules, you'll never rule".

When it comes to parliamentary procedure, a little knowledge goes a long way. But without that knowledge you're likely to end up getting "run over" – at least in settings where these rules apply. But if you take the time to learn, you can use that knowledge for the rest of your life as an activist, (or just as a concerned citizen). In general, the purpose of parliamentary procedure is to bring order to argument, as well as to protect the rights of the minority. Through a sensible use of the rules you can delay action to try and force a compromise, get a proposal dropped all-together, or try to put an issue off until a later date when you've had time to lobby others or make sure you can turn out more supporters.

Getting Comfortable with the Rules

...knowledge = confidence

Parliamentary procedure only *sounds* intimidating. It really isn't. A lot of people who have been in politics for a long time tend to run their meetings as formally as possible with very stiff-sounding parliamentary motions and very little explanation. Why? Because it intimidates people who are new to the process, and helps keep the agenda in the hands of the establishment. This guide is to get you comfortable enough to ask questions, participate in debate, and offer your own motions. The more knowledge and confidence you have with the rules, the more successful you'll be.

Almost every organization you will encounter is generally run according to *Robert's Rules of Order: Newly Revised,* (and it is usually designated as the parliamentary authority in the group's constitution and/or bylaws). The group's rules define operating procedures and the rights of the membership. Make sure to ask for a copy.

If you don't already have a copy of *Robert's Rules*, click here and get a copy from Amazon, (or click here for the "Robert's Rules for Dummies" version!). Get familiar with it. Don't be intimidated by its size, because most of it is just commentary on the basics. The first pages to read are the ones printed in a different color in the middle. These pages have useful charts for remembering difficult concepts, a prioritized listing of motions, things to know about them and even several pages describing how to say things in a way that make you sound

53

like you've done this before. Second, flip to the back of *Robert's Rules* and review the index. Here you can quickly locate the pages covering situations you may find yourself in; whether dealing with elections, balloting, meetings, motions or agendas. As you learn more, make notes in the index to direct you to the sections you use the most – or are most likely to use in the future, so you can find help when you need it.

Meeting Agendas

...I suppose you're all wondering why I called this meeting

Meetings should proceed with a pre-set agenda. The role of a presiding officer, (usually a chairman), is to ensure that the meeting proceeds on time and on topic. If the meeting strays from the agenda, or if something is done that is not fair, or if debate turns to personal attacks, any member can call this to the attention of the chair by calling out "Point of order!" and requesting that the chair restore order.

A good agenda will include specific reference to items that the chair knows or believes will be raised at the meeting, (such as elections, adoption of a budget, etc.). Voting on a motion to adopt an agenda is one of the first orders of business of any meeting and it is adopted by a simple majority vote. Once an agenda is adopted however, it takes a 2/3's vote to change it. If you're running a meeting, make sure that the things that are important to you are placed strategically, (meaning early, if you're supporters are there and might have to leave early...or late, if your support is weak and you hope some of your opposition goes home!). If you're not running the meeting, pay attention to the proposed agenda before it's adopted. You can move to amend it (with a simple majority vote) before it's adopted, for the same reasons listed above. If it's adopted and you wish to make a change later, you could request unanimous consent to take up your agenda item out of order. If there is an objection, it will then take a 2/3's vote to amend it. Or you could also try and move to "table" consideration of any intervening items on the agenda.

Agendas not only help keep your meetings on track, but as a result they can help keep them from becoming deathly boring. There's nothing like boring meetings to keep people form coming back!

Visit my website at DrewMcKissick.com ~ Connect on Twitter @DrewMcKissick

WHAT TO INCLUDE IN AN AGENDA

The following is a list of items you might see in a typical agenda, (and the order they would usually appear):

- *Call to order and Invocation*

- *Adoption of the Agenda*

- *Reading and Approval of Minutes:* The minutes are summarized notes of what happened at the last meeting. Minutes are legally binding records of the organization, and are used to prove various actions that are taken. If the minutes as read are not accurate, they should be corrected from the floor.

- *Reports of Officers, Boards, and Standing Committees:* These may include such items as a Treasurer's report or reports of committees established in the bylaws of the organization.

- *Reports of Special Committees:* These are committees not in the bylaws but appointed by the organization in a previous meeting.

- *Special Orders:* Items of business that were designated as "special orders" at a previous meeting to make sure that it gets discussed at the next meeting.

- *Old Business and General Orders:* Old business is items that have carried over from the previous meeting as a result of adjourning without completing its business. General orders are issues which have been made in order for the present meeting but not been designated as special orders.

- *New Business:* New scheduled matters items from the floor.

- *Adjourn*

Quorums

...where is everyone?

You gotta' have people to have a meeting – or at least "enough" people. In order to conduct business, a meeting should have at least the minimum number of members necessary as defined in the bylaws. This minimum number is called a "quorum" and protects against having any unrepresentative action taken in the name of the group. In most cases when a quorum is not present and a vote looks likely to go against a particular side, someone on that side will "call for a quorum". If a count indicates that there is no quorum present, then no binding business can be done and the group must adjourn.

The point being that you always want to make sure "your" people are present. Let the other guys worry about a quorum and whether or not "their" people are there. But, if you're short of supporters, take a quick count and make sure a quorum is present. If not, move to adjourn the meeting for lack of a quorum.

Making Motions

...mother may I?

In general, only one person may speak at a time, (otherwise it's a mob). The presiding officer (or chairman) controls the flow of debate by "recognizing" individual members. Raising a hand is usually sufficient to be recognized, but sometimes it may be necessary to call out "Mr. Chairman" in order to be recognized, (or even stand up…whatever it takes). Once recognized, a member can make any number of motions. If a motion is not appropriate for the given time, the chairman may rule the motion "out of order", which prevents the motion from being considered on the floor. If that's the case, ask when it would be in order. If it is in order, the chairman generally asks, "Is there a second?", as most motions require a second person to support it in order for debate to go forward. Without a second, the motion dies. Be prepared by having a second supporter lined up to support your motions.

After a question has been moved and seconded, the chairman will repeat the motion and ask if there is any discussion. If so, then let the debate begin! If not, the motion will be put to an immediate vote. Most motions are debatable. During debate, the chairman should recognize the maker of the motion, who will explain reasons to vote for it. The chairman should then try to alternate between opponents and proponents of the motion.

AMENDING MOTIONS

Most motions can be amended at any time during debate. But amendments can only "amend" in one place, meaning you can't have an amendment change multiple places in a motion at once. And once text has been amended it cannot be amended again. However, you can use the "bigger bite rule" and grab all of the previously amended area along with some extra text (on the front or the back), making a "bigger bite". Then you can either "strike" (delete words), "insert" (add words), or "strike and insert" (do both at the same time), to get your proposed text to read the way you wish.

Amendments are moved, seconded, and debated just as motions are. If the amendment passes, the chairman re-states the motion as amended. If the amendment fails, the motion is then open for amendment again or for a vote on the main motion. Generally, debate ends when someone moves to "call the previous question", (basically, a fancy way to say "let's stop talking and start voting"), and that motion passes with a 2/3's vote. (Rule of thumb: most motions require a mere majority to pass, but any motion that would restrict the rights of others – such as cutting off debate when others still want to be heard – requires a larger majority).

VOTING ON MOTIONS

Voting is generally done by a voice vote in most groups, (calling for the "ayes" and "nays"). If there is doubt about the outcome, call out "division!" for a standing vote (people standing up as the "ayes and nays" are called for). Paper ballots or a roll call may also be requested, but can slow things down, (and sometimes upset people who are ready to leave). That's also something to keep in mind when it comes to what's in your best interest, (a slow meeting or a fast meeting).

> **REMEMBER:** *In election situations, if nominations are taken from the floor of the assembly, you don't need to wait to be recognized, (and no second is usually required). An individual can be nominated for any number of offices at the same time. If a nominating committee formally nominates candidates under your group's bylaws, it's still possible to nominate candidates from the floor under Robert's Rules.*

PRECEDENCE OF MOTIONS

Some motions are more important than others. Over the years, a system of precedence of motions has evolved which permits various motions to be offered while other motions are still pending before an assembly. There are three classes of motions: "main motions", "subsidiary motions", and "privileged motions".

The *main motion* is the basis of all parliamentary procedure and provides a means of bringing business before the group for consideration. As the lowest ranking motion, it can only be considered when no other business is pending.

Subsidiary motions are those which may be applied to another motion in order to modify it, delay action, or kill it altogether. Subsidiary motions rank higher than main motions, but lower than privileged motions.

Privileged motions, as you can guess, are the highest ranking motions. All other motions yield to them. While they may have no relation to the pending question like subsidiary motions, their priority entitles them to immediate consideration. The five privileged motions relate to the rights of members and to the organization, rather than to particular items of business.

As the table below shows, each motion takes precedence over those motions in the table below it and yields to those above it. For example, while a main motion is pending, a motion to amend may be offered. Since the motion to amend takes precedence over the main motion in the table, the assembly turns its attention to the motion to amend while the main motion is still on the floor.

Motion	Type	Debatable?	Need 2nd?	Vote
Fix the time to adjourn	Privileged	No	Yes	Majority
Adjourn	Privileged	No	Yes	Majority
Recess	Privileged	No	Yes	Majority
Raise a question of privilege	Privileged	No	No	n/a
Call for the orders of the day	Privileged	No	No	n/a
Lay on the table	Subsidiary	No	Yes	Majority
Previous question	Subsidiary	No	Yes	2/3's
Limit or extend debate	Subsidiary	No	Yes	2/3's
Postpone to a time certain	Subsidiary	Yes	Yes	Majority
Commit (or Refer)	Subsidiary	Yes	Yes	Majority
Amend	Subsidiary	Yes	Yes	Majority
Postpone indefinitely	Subsidiary	Yes	Yes	Majority
Main motion	n/a	Yes	Yes	Majority

(Above table taken from Robert's Rules of Order: Newly Revised, 9th Edition)

STRATEGIC CONSIDERATIONS

Contentious issues can easily become complicated from a procedural standpoint. Surely you've been at a meeting that got bogged down in parliamentary procedure because people were debating something controversial. There can be main motions, amendments to a motion, substitute amendments, and secondary amendments. So how do you protect your position? Generally, go for an early test vote on something that's important to your group. Early votes on an important point are good ways to frame the debate and get everyone on the record – especially if you have a roll call vote, (which makes it harder for others to

58

"flip-flop" and may also reveal unknown allies or opponents). <u>It's a good rule of thumb to always have a partner (or even partners) to work with in a group setting using parliamentary procedure.</u> This ensures support in offering and seconding motions, speaking up in debate and keeping a watch on the proceedings (and your potential supporters). Plus it's good for moral support, as nobody really likes to be in the middle of controversy alone.

Training for the Future

...the more you know, the luckier you get

If you have a group of people that would like more serious training in parliamentary procedure, a good place to start would be to contact friendly elected officials that have had a good bit of experience. You could even hire a professional parliamentarian to conduct a training session, or inquire about seminars. Those who want to take it a step further can take official courses and seek parliamentary certification from a national organization. <u>The bottom line is the more conservative local activists there are who have this type of experience, the better for the conservative movement as a whole.</u>

For more information, contact the National Association of Parliamentarians. You can visit their website here.

Parliamentary Procedure Review:

- ***Get comfortable with the rules.*** *Study the highlights and don't let it intimidate you!*

- ***Know the agenda.*** *And if you're running a meeting, always have one.*

- ***Have a partner.*** *Moral support means confidence.*

- ***Get training.*** *A little knowledge goes a long way!*

SECTION 5: VOLUNTEER MANAGEMENT

"Volunteers are at least worth what you pay them"

American public policy is moved by its citizens. Again, it's all about people. People work for candidates in their campaigns, cast ballots on Election Day, and lobby those elected officials to help shape public policy once they get into office. And, given that so few people actually do participate in the political process, just a few willing volunteers can have a dramatic impact.

From a conservative grassroots standpoint, the goal is to build a volunteer network that can change our political environment by participating in political parties, helping good candidates get elected, and expressing support for conservative ideals. Without their support, nothing happens. But building a network of willing volunteers requires management skills different from those used with employees. Since the vast bulk of political work is done by volunteers, it is important that leaders at all levels understand some basic principles of volunteer management. The following are some general principles that you should keep in mind.

SHARE THE VISION

Do your volunteers know the vision? Don't assume willing volunteers understand how your group operates and why. Share the vision so they will understand what the goals are and how they can help achieve them. Clearly communicating the vision creates a spirit of unity and purpose, and good leaders will always make an effort to motivate those that they have recruited by keeping them focused on the importance of the cause they are involved in. Without a vision, there is no leadership.

KEEP IT SIMPLE

It seems that the more complicated a plan is, the more the planners tend to like it. The idea being that, if it is big, intricate, complicated, and virtually impossible to understand, then it *must* be a great plan. In grassroots organizing nothing could be further from the truth. Complex plans usually fail because they have too many moving parts, too many places where they can fail and are too difficult to understand, implement and fix. On the other hand, a simple plan makes it easier for volunteers to see how they fit in, and how what they do makes a difference and helps accomplish the overall mission.

So remember the KISS method, ("keep it simple, stupid").

60

BE A LEADER

One of the most important rules is never to ask someone to do a job you wouldn't do yourself. Building and maintaining a grassroots organization can require a lot of "grunt work", which means a lot of volunteers and a lot of hours. <u>If you're going to get the most out of a team, then they need to know that you're a part of the team as well.</u> Show them how the job is done and that you're willing to pitch in to help do it.

AIM FOR SUCCESS

Grassroots organizing is inherently "messy" because it involves people. (Remember, politics is people) And people can behave in all kinds of funny ways, which impacts how well you're able to get things done. In other words, for the sake of your own sanity, you have to recognize that things will never be perfect. In fact, trying to be a perfectionist will likely leave you short of your goals and missing out on many opportunities. There is limited time, resources and volunteers in order to get most of the things done that need to be accomplished. <u>Don't stress so much on one area that you're never able to address the other things that need doing.</u>

Ultimately, this is all about making sure conservatives are represented in the political process. You can't let the small details get in the way of the big picture. <u>Your job is not to run a perfect operation, but rather to create an something outmaneuver and "out hustle" the opposition.</u> Remember the old saying, "the best is the enemy of the good".

Volunteer Management Review:

- **Share the vision.** *Explain the goal and how they can help achieve it.*

- **Keep things simple.** *Make the plan focused and easy to understand.*

- **Be a servant / leader.** *Let them know you're willing to get your hands dirty.*

- **Aim for success...not perfection.** *Focus on the big picture.*

61

PASS IT ON

"Pass on what you have learned." - Yoda

Politics is a game of numbers. Whoever has the most usually wins. As a result, <u>one of the most important functions of any grassroots leader is to recruit others to their cause by identifying those who share their beliefs and concerns.</u> But the job doesn't end there. It also involves taking those likeminded citizens and teaching them how to effectively engage in the political process and remove the mystery that surrounds it.

The more knowledge a new recruit has the more confidence they will have and the more effective they will become. And just as every good leader should work to identify and train their successors, <u>every grassroots leader should work to identify and train the next generation of leadership</u>. To educate them on what you've learned about the political process and how to be effective.

While you've surely seen local activists go on to become elected officials at various levels, what's not always evident is the political education and training of the volunteers that made those campaigns successful – and the past leaders that recruited them to the cause.

<u>The success of the conservative agenda hangs on bringing new people into the process, and then promoting them up the ladder and into the system.</u> And you're a part of that process.

Welcome to the farm team!

Did you find this book useful?
If so, let others know about it! Send them an email and tell them to visit Grassroots101 so they can get a copy of this and/or other resources to become more effectively involved in our political system.

Also, be sure to join the email list at DrewMcKissick.com to receive news about updates and new resources! Connect with me on Twitter @DrewMcKissick.

Conservative Organizations & Resources

If you're already involved with a group, that's great. But if you are not, consider linking up with a nationally based group that already has some resources that you can draw from. They will be glad to have you!

American Conservative Union
703-836-8602
www.conservative.org

American Enterprise Institute
202-862-5800
www.aei.org

American Family Association
662-844-5036
www.afa.net

American Legislative Exchange
202-466-3800
www.alec.org

Americans for Tax Reform
202-785-0266
www.atr.org

Concerned Women for America
202-488-7000
www.cwfa.org

Christian Coalition of America
202-479-6900
www.cc.org

Club for Growth
202-955-5500
www.clubforgrowth.org

Conservative Outpost
www.ConservativeOutpost.com

Eagle Forum
618-462-5415
www.eagleforum.org

Family Research Council
202-393-2100
www.frc.org

Free Congress Foundation
202-546-3000
www.freecongress.org

Freedom Works
888-564-6273
www.freedomworks.org

Friedman Foundation
www.friedmanfoundation.org

The Heritage Foundation
202-546-4400
www.heritage.org

The Leadership Institute
703-247-2000
www.leadershipinstitute.org

Media Research Center
703-683-9733
www.mediaresearch.org

Natl Center for Public Policy
202-543-4110
www.nationalcenter.org

National Right to Life
202-626-8800
www.nrlc.org

National Right to Work Committee
800-325-7892
www.right-to-work.org

Rutherford Institute
804-978-3888
www.rutherford.org

Republican National Committee
202-863-8630
www.gop.com

Tradition Values Coalition
202-547-8570
www.traditionalvalues.org

www.ingramcontent.com/pod-product-compliance
Lightning Source LLC
Chambersburg PA
CBHW060816270326
41930CB00002B/57